THE
NEANDERTHAL
BOOK

S0-AQI-857

By Stephen Cumbaa & Kathlyn Stewart

Illustrated by Kim La Fave

Workman Publishing
New York

Cumbaa, Stephen.
    The Neanderthal book/by Stephen Cumbaa and Kathlyn Stewart;
illustrated by Kim La Fave.
        p.   cm.
    "A Somerville House book."
    Summary: A guide to who the Neanderthals were, when they first
appeared, where they settled, how they lived, and why they disappeared. Includes a bone-by-bone study of the Neanderthal skeleton,
projects, and activities.
    ISBN 0-7611-0904-8 (paperback)
    1. Neanderthals—Juvenile literature.   [1. Neanderthals.
2. Prehistoric peoples.]   I. Stewart, Kathlyn.   II. La Fave, Kim, ill.
III. Title.
    GN285.C85   1997
    569.9—dc21   97-40108
                                                      CIP
                                                       AC

Workman books are available at special discounts when purchased in
bulk for premiums and sales promotions as well as for fund-raising or
educational use. Special editions or book excerpts can also be created
to specification. For details, contact the Special Sales Director at the
address below.

Workman Publishing
708 Broadway
New York, NY 10003-9555

Manufactured in the United States of America
First printing October 1997
10   9   8   7   6   5   4   3   2

Contents

Meet the Neanderthals!

The mystery of the Neanderthals begins with the discovery of some human bones that had been buried in a cave for thousands of years. When this partial skeleton was studied along with similar bones found at other locations, scientists came to the amazing conclusion that a separate human species once inhabited the continent of Europe and parts of Asia.

"**Neanderthal Man**" was named for the German valley (*thal*) of *Neander*, where he was unearthed in 1856. In modern German, the word for "valley" is written without the "h" (*tal*), so some scientists now spell the name *Neandertal*.

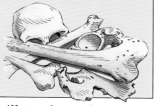

What happened to these early people? We call them Neanderthals, or *Homo neanderthalensis*, but who were they? What did they look like, and where did they come from? Above all, how did they manage to survive for more than 200,000 years?

This book and skeleton will teach you how to search for answers to these questions in the bones they left behind. The Neanderthal flint-point spearhead and bone flute also hold clues to one of the greatest mysteries in human history.

The human beings called Neanderthals may turn out to be more like us than we ever imagined.

A FAMILY ALBUM

Today, we know the Neanderthals were just one of many species of humans, or hominids. The information gathered from the skeletal remains of these early humans gives us a picture of people in prehistoric habitats and helps us to understand our own evolution.

The First Bipeds

Scientists can now be almost certain that Neanderthals and modern humans have a common ancestor—a group of hominids belonging to the genus *Australopithecus*, or "southern ape." These small creatures with long, powerful arms first appeared in Africa well over four million years ago and developed into separate species such as *A. africanus* and *A. afarensis*. They probably lived partly in trees, but what made them different from other primates was their ability to walk upright on two feet. This erect posture, called bipedalism, enabled them to look out over tall savanna grass and use their hands for gathering

Little Lucy

One of the first *Australopithecus* skeletons ever found was nicknamed Lucy. Full-grown but only about the size of a modern human 10-year-old child, Lucy lived in the Rift Valley of East Africa more than three million years ago. She

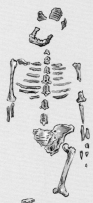

may have spent some of her time in trees, but her skeletal formation tells us that she could also walk upright.

Only two-thirds of Lucy's skeleton was recovered in 1974. The skeleton's official name is AL 288-1.

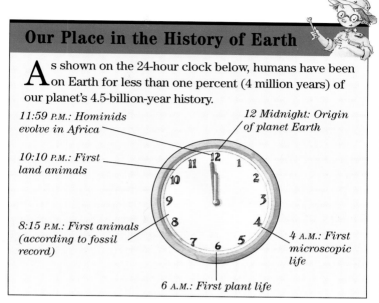

Our Place in the History of Earth

As shown on the 24-hour clock below, humans have been on Earth for less than one percent (4 million years) of our planet's 4.5-billion-year history.

11:59 P.M.: Hominids evolve in Africa

12 Midnight: Origin of planet Earth

10:10 P.M.: First land animals

8:15 P.M.: First animals (according to fossil record)

4 A.M.: First microscopic life

6 A.M.: First plant life

leaves and fruit, birds' eggs and even flying ants. It also subjected less body surface to the hot sun overhead while exposing more skin to cooling breezes.

"Upright Man"

A little over two million years ago, a new genus classified as *Homo* evolved from the australopithecines in Africa. *Homo habilis*, or "Handy Man," was taller than the first hominids, had a larger brain and made simple tools. But it was *Homo erectus*, or "Upright Man," who began to show true advances in human development. Members of this species had a brain about two-thirds the size of ours (but twice the size of a chimpanzee's) and probably communicated in a "language" of grunting sounds. Their jaws and teeth show that they were meat-eaters, while their long limbs and narrow hips indicate that they were built for speed. They made more sophisticated tools than *H. habilis* and were probably the first of our ancestors to use fire.

Out of Africa

Recent fossil finds show that members of the *Homo erectus* species made their way north out of Africa and spread out across the Old World. In Europe, over 230,000 years ago, some of these early humans evolved into the early people who would come to be known as Neanderthals. As their bodies adapted to the climates of the Ice Age, they developed heavy bones and powerful muscles that helped them survive in brutal environments. For the next 200,000 years, they roamed as far north as England and as far south as the Rock of Gibraltar on the Mediterranean coast. They also expanded into southwest Asia and the Middle East, always on the move through frozen tundra and barren wilderness.

> In 1997, DNA was extracted from an arm bone of the original Neanderthal skeleton. This amazing scientific feat proved once and for all that Neanderthals and modern human beings do not share the same genes—even though they belong to the same family tree.

But even before the Neanderthals first appeared, other members of *Homo erectus* were evolving into *Homo sapiens*—our own species. Thus it's very possible that three different branches of the human family were living at nearly the same time in the same part of the world!

Homo sapiens, or "Wise Men," would keep the slimmer stature of *H. erectus* and develop larger brains until, at least 100,000 years ago, they emerged as modern human beings.

Neanderthal   Homo sapiens

Close Relatives

Forty thousand years ago, groups of *Homo sapiens* arrived in Europe—where isolated bands of Neanderthals were still struggling to survive. Whether or not the two species ever met up with each other is another unsolved mystery of our ancient past.

Members of Homo sapiens, *our own species, are the only human beings alive today.*

The earliest Neanderthals appeared in Europe more than 230,000 years ago. By about 30,000 years ago, the species had vanished from the earth.

Archaic Homo sapiens, *the direct ancestor of modern human beings, first appeared about 800,000 years ago.*

Homo erectus *evolved in Africa almost 2 million years ago.*

PUTTING IT ALL TOGETHER

The scientists who look for ancient bones need knowledge, patience—and luck. Called paleontologists, these dedicated fossil-seekers examine the surface of the earth for clues and then begin to dig into the ground if a site looks promising. When bones are found, tiny brushes and dental picks are used to clear away the dirt so they can be closely studied.

A complete Neanderthal skeleton has yet to be found, but the earth has yielded bones from hundreds of individuals—including men, women, children and even a 10-month-old baby. From these remains, paleontologists have succeeded in constructing a model skeleton to create a head-to-toe Neanderthal portrait. And by assembling the skeleton that comes with this book, you, too, can help shed new light on our cousins of long ago.

Paleontologists look for clues in ancient Neanderthal bones. No matter how small, each new clue fills in another part of the puzzle.

The Bone Map

The bones that come with this book are based on fossilized Neanderthal bones. The bones fit together and can be popped into place to form an accurate model of an adult Neanderthal skeleton.

The flint-point spear and bone flute complete your set of clues. When not in use, the Neanderthal model skeleton can stay on display in its own see-through case.

1. Front of skull
2. Upper rear skull
3. Lower rear skull
4. Jaw
5. Right collarbone
6. Left collarbone
7. Right shoulder blade
8. Left shoulder blade
9. Left upper arm
10. Right upper arm
11. Left lower arm
12. Right lower arm
13. Left hand
14. Right hand
15. Spine
16. Right rib cage
17. Left rib cage
18. Left pelvis
19. Right pelvis
20. Left upper leg
21. Right upper leg
22. Left lower leg
23. Right lower leg
24. Right foot
25. Left foot
26. Flute
27. Spear
28. Stand
29. Stand clip

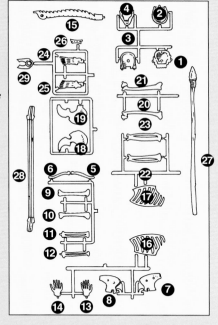

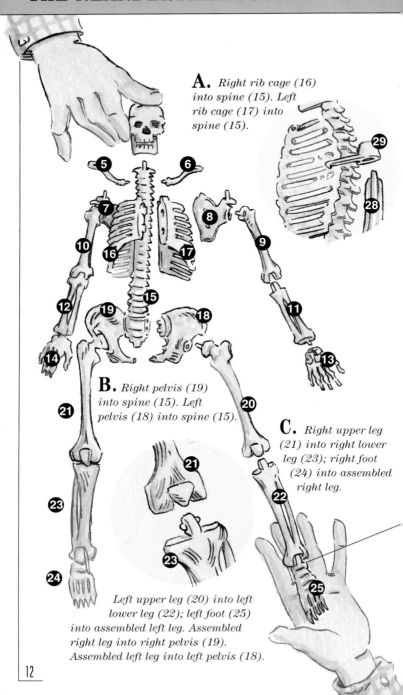

A. *Right rib cage (16) into spine (15). Left rib cage (17) into spine (15).*

B. *Right pelvis (19) into spine (15). Left pelvis (18) into spine (15).*

C. *Right upper leg (21) into right lower leg (23); right foot (24) into assembled right leg.*

Left upper leg (20) into left lower leg (22); left foot (25) into assembled left leg. Assembled right leg into right pelvis (19). Assembled left leg into left pelvis (18).

12

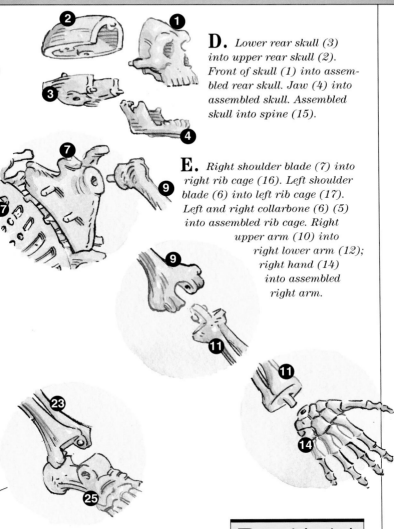

D. *Lower rear skull (3) into upper rear skull (2). Front of skull (1) into assembled rear skull. Jaw (4) into assembled skull. Assembled skull into spine (15).*

E. *Right shoulder blade (7) into right rib cage (16). Left shoulder blade (6) into left rib cage (17). Left and right collarbone (6) (5) into assembled rib cage. Right upper arm (10) into right lower arm (12); right hand (14) into assembled right arm.*

eft upper arm (9) into left lower arm (11); t hand (13) into assembled left arm. ssembled left arm into left shoulder blade). Assembled right arm into right shoulder ade (8). Stand clip (29) into assembled rib ge. Base (28) into clip (29).

Be sure to keep track of left and right. When the Neanderthal skeleton is facing you, its left side will appear to be on the right—and vice versa.

WHAT'S THE DIFFERENCE?

Looking at Bones

L ike the modern human skelelton, the Neanderthal skeleton provided a flexible framework for muscles and organs. But the Neanderthal bones recovered from "digs" tend to show their great age. Usually stained by minerals in the soil, they're often broken or cracked from thousands of years of trampling, rockfalls and changes in temperature and humidity.

The skeleton that comes with this book reflects these fossil characteristics. Look carefully for cracks in the bones as well as small depressions along the edges. The long bones of the arms and legs in particular show many of the signs of age that paleontologists encounter in their finds.

Cracks and other signs of age are common in Neanderthal bones.

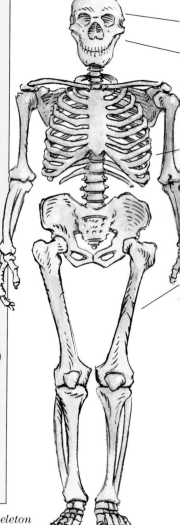

Neanderthal skeleton

The top of the Neanderthal skull was flatter than ours, leaving less room for the forehead.

A thick ridge of bone jutted out like an awning above large, round eyes.

The cheeks and long jaw swept back from a nose that was much bigger than ours and helped to regulate body temperature.

The Neanderthal's broad shoulders and rib cage provided a sturdy frame for heavy-duty muscles.

Like all other joints, the elbow joint was wider than ours because the bones were bigger and knobbier at the ends.

Even the shafts of Neanderthal bones were thicker than ours, requiring massive muscles to lift and move them.

The Neanderthal skeleton reflects the physical adaptations needed for survival in the extreme cold of the Great Ice Age. Overall, Neanderthal bodies were shorter than ours and thicker through the middle—perfectly suited for storing up heat.

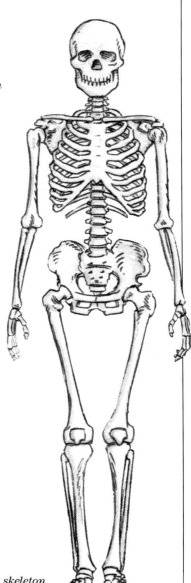

Modern human skeleton

BONE-CHILLING TIMES

Neanderthal bones are found in soil that dates all the way back to the Great Ice Age. Over a million years ago, ice sheets crept over the northern reaches of Europe, Asia and North America. From that date until about 10,000 years ago, the earth warmed up several times but then cooled down again over long stretches known as *glacial periods*. Between two such cold stretches, during an *interglacial period*, the Neanderthals appeared in Europe. But then the cold returned, locking early humans out of the northern parts of the continent. We have almost no record of the Neanderthals from 180,000 to 130,000 years ago, when relative warmth was

During the Ice Age, the whole world grew cooler than it is now, but it wasn't a time of permanent winter everywhere. In fact, the temperatures of the hot areas of today may have been very pleasant back then.

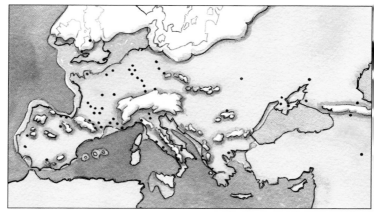

PWhen ice covered northern Europe and Asia during the last glacial period, lower sea levels altered the shorelines of the two continents (see pink shaded areas). Black circles represent important sites where Neanderthal remains have been found.

Dating Deposits

How do we know that Neanderthals lived in Europe almost 200,000 years before modern humans joined them there? And how can anyone be sure they were still alive only 30,000 years ago? One answer lies in the soil deposits where Neanderthal bones have been discovered. Two methods of dating these deposits are based on radio-active mineral decay. Uranium, for example, turns to lead at a predictable rate, so we can tell how long ago the decaying process began. In volcanic deposits, we can also measure the decay of potassium into a gas called argon.

Another dating method tests the electrons trapped in deposits that were once exposed to heat from the sun. By measuring the light emitted by the remaining electrons, we can calculate how much time has gone by since the deposits were first buried.

Radiocarbon dating is one of the few methods based on the fossils themselves. All living things contain carbon, which disintegrates at a known rate when they die. By assessing the carbon found in a fossil, we can determine almost exactly how long ago death occurred—but only if the person, animal or plant lived within the past 50,000 years.

restored to the earth and they emerged fully adapted to the rigorous life of the Ice Age.

About 100,000 years ago, the last glacial period began and the Neanderthals spent much of their time on the cold fringes of ice sheets a mile and a half thick. In this hostile environment, with plant life and wild animals in short supply, they survived until about 30,000 years ago—just 20,000 years before the final thaw.

Is the Ice Age over? It's possible that we're living in the midst of an interglacial period. Thousands of years from now, the earth may freeze up again with temperatures like those experienced by the Neanderthals.

Life on the Edge

For thousands of years, the early Neanderthals dominated the continent of Europe, making their way across the bleak landscapes on the glaciers' southern rim. Traveling in small clusters, many of them may have spent their entire lives without crossing the path of other Neanderthals. In fact, scientists estimate that their population at any given time probably numbered only in the tens of thousands.

Wrapped in animal skins, they set out from their temporary shelters in caves or under rock ledges to search the land for food. In winter, plant life was reduced to a bare minimum, so they

depended mainly on the meat of wild animals that roamed the northern tundras. And always in the wings, quietly alert, waited the hungry foxes and wolves that competed with them for survival in this unforgiving environment.

GIANTS OF THE ICE AGE

South of the ice sheets, in the shadow of glaciers, life went on despite the bitter cold. The Neanderthals' world was filled with many animals whose descendants are still around today—rhinoceros, antelope, bison and badgers, as well as sheep and reindeer. But the Ice Age also boasted some of the largest land mammals the world has ever known.

Woolly mammoths grew 11 feet tall at the shoulder and used their long curving tusks to defend themselves

The woolly rhinoceros charged with great speed and attacked with two lethal front horns. Cave bears were bigger than modern grizzly bears, but were vegetarians. Like bears today they were unpredictable and could attack or defend themselves with sharp teeth and claws. Packs of wolves and other hungry animals—wild dogs and bone-crushing hyenas—also patrolled the tundra looking for food.

Even some of the deer were giants —larger than today's moose— with antlers spreading 12 feet from tip to tip.

So fierce were the predators of the Ice Age that smaller animals hid from them in burrows or huddled together in timid herds. Neanderthals were vulnerable to attack as well, but they had their stone weapons to defend themselves. Even so, these primitive weapons would be no match against a raging woolly rhinoceros or a cave lion on the prowl, and they had to learn the animals' habits in order to hunt in their territory or keep out of their way.

The dangerous cave lions of Europe were larger than the African lions of today, with thick coats of fur for protection against the cold.

Awesome Adversaries

The Neanderthals hunted ferocious wild oxen called aurochs, the ancestors of our modern cows. Like most of the giant mammals of the Ice Age, the auroch is now extinct. As the climate changed, perhaps their food supply died off. Or perhaps our own ancestors killed them all or crowded them out. The real answer is probably a combination of the two.

Six feet tall at the shoulder, with long, sharp horns, the auroch demanded not only courage but careful planning among bands of hunters.

BONE BY BONE

Even though the Neanderthals didn't leave a written history of their lives, we have a record of bone and stone that scientists can read. Often bone fossils are the only clues in the story, although tools and other artifacts found nearby may tell their own tales.

What's a Fossil?

Fossils are the remains of animals and plants that have been preserved by nature. Unfortunately for us, only a tiny fraction of human bones survive as fossils that can be studied by paleontologists. Dinosaur bones, which date back at least 65 million years, are found completely fossilized. Fossilization

Examined through a microscope, thin slices of Neanderthal bone show closely packed mineral crystals. In contrast, bone slices from modern humans reveal a looser pattern of crystals, indicating less strength in the bone.

of Neanderthal bones is often incomplete, and scientists must make do with bits and pieces of skeletons.

1. Conditions have to be just right for bones to become fossils. For example, if a Neanderthal died trying to cross a flooded stream, his body might then be covered by mud and buried in sediment.

2. Over time, the soft body tissues would disintegrate and water would seep into the bones, replacing parts of them with minerals from the earth.

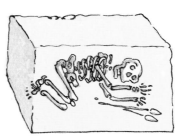

New Bones, Old Bones

O ur bones are living tissues that continue growing after we're born. Inside the bones, some cells form the marrow that produces red blood cells; others create a mesh that fills with spaces of minerals to make the bone hard and stiff.

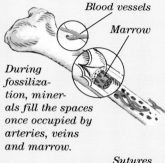

Blood vessels

Marrow

During fossilization, minerals fill the spaces once occupied by arteries, veins and marrow.

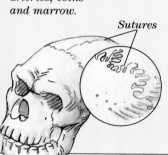

Sutures

Knowing how bones grow can tell scientists a lot about fossil bones. For example, the end of the thighbone doesn't fuse completely to the shaft until the teenage years, so early age can be identified.

Similar clues in the bones of Neanderthals show that most of them died young. Only about one in every 10 lived to be older than age 35.

The skull plates meet at places called sutures, which are not fully fused until the very late years of adulthood. The stage of fusion can help determine the age at which a person died.

3. *If this process continued undisturbed, the bones of the skeleton would become fossils and might even, as the soil eroded, appear on the surface of the earth to be examined by paleontologists.*

THE SKULL

One of the first things you notice about the skull of a Neanderthal is the heavy brow ridge above the eye sockets. The low, sloping forehead accentuates this massive ridge, which no doubt provided protection for the face. The brow may also have supported powerful jaw muscles that allowed Neanderthals to eat particularly tough bits of meat and to clamp sizable objects between their teeth. The swept-back cheekbones on either side of the large nasal cavity are another distinctive feature of the Neanderthal skull.

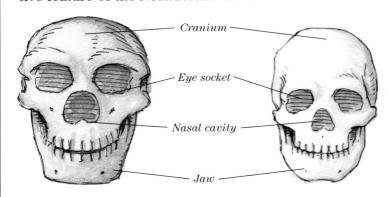

The skull is composed of bones that protect the brain and form the face. The Neanderthal skull (at left) is wider than the modern human skull (right), marked by cavernous eye and nose cavities, and squared off at the jaw.

Big Brains

Neanderthal brains were larger than ours; in fact, they're the largest brains on record for a human species. But do bigger brains mean higher intelligence? The answer is no. Comparisons of intelligence are made according to the relative shape and size of different parts of the brain. For example, the frontal lobes of the cerebrum, responsible for thought, speech and cre-

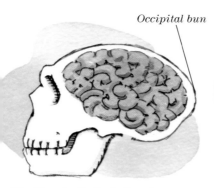

Occipital bun

The Neanderthal's skull and brain were flatter and longer from front to back. The "occipital bun" at the back anchored mighty neck muscles.

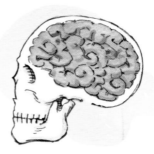

The higher modern human forehead protects the large frontal lobes of the brain, where most of our thinking is done.

ativity, are large in the modern human brain but less developed in the model of a Neanderthal brain. On the other hand, larger lobes at the rear of the brain, where visual images are processed, suggest that the Neanderthals may have had better eyesight than ours.

Casts made from the inside surface of Neanderthal skulls show that the occipital lobe of the brain's left hemisphere was larger than the one on the right side. Since most modern human beings with a larger left occipital lobe are right-handed, researchers believe Neanderthals were mostly right-handed, too. This conclusion is bolstered by evidence that their right arm was stronger than the left.

Measuring with Mustard Seeds

How do scientists estimate the size and shape of the Neanderthal's brain? One way is to fill up a skull with mustard seeds or raw rice, then pour the seeds into a cylinder that measures how much space would be taken up by the brain.

GRIPPING JAWS

Neanderthal jawbones and teeth can tell us a lot about their world—what they ate, how they chewed, even how they used their jaws as a vise.

From the shape of the teeth, we know that the Neanderthals were omnivorous and capable of chewing everything from tough meat to stringy roots and stems. It seems they used the sharp incisors in front for biting and tearing and the molars at the back for crushing and grinding food. Sadly, the evidence indicates that many Neanderthal teeth did not develop properly—a sign that starvation was an all-too-common threat.

Neanderthal teeth were larger and longer than ours. Worn, rounded-off edges show that the teeth were often used for gripping and grasping.

The shape of the jawbone positioned the teeth in a U-shaped curve, rather than in the more rounded bowl shape of modern human teeth, and most chewing took place toward the front of the mouth. But the most outstanding difference is *how* the Neanderthals chewed. While we move our lower jaw up and down when we chew, they moved their jaw from side to side.

Like modern humans, Neanderthal children had 20 "baby teeth" that gradually fell out and were replaced by a set of 32 adult teeth. This fact helps paleontologists figure out the age of individual Neanderthals when they died.

Mysterious Scratches

Parallel scratches have been seen in the hard enamel covering of many Neanderthal front teeth. Scientists think these marks were most likely made by sharp stone tools. Long, fibery plant parts and unwieldy pieces of meat would need slicing before they could be eaten, and it appears that Neanderthals used sharpened stones as knives to cut their food into bite-size pieces—not on a plate, but at mouth level!

A Third Hand

Neanderthals probably used their powerful jaws to grip animal skins or pieces of wood while they worked on them. They might clamp down on the hide of a deer, for example, to hold it in place and leave their hands free for the job of scraping it clean. Afterward, they might even chew on the hide to make it soft enough to wear as clothing.

Powered by huge muscles, the Neanderthal jaw could clasp heavy objects in a secure, vise-like grip between clenched teeth.

Food on the Fire

Fire not only provided warmth and kept wild animals at bay, but also gave the Neanderthals a way to heat up or dry out their food. In fact, the secret of making fire was often the key to survival. The first Neanderthals probably rubbed two dry sticks together or rotated wooden sticks called "fire drills" between their hands into dry grass and pieces of tinder on the ground. Striking a piece of flint against another rock was a fire-starting method of the later Stone Age.

Neanderthals needed lots of calories to fuel their thick, heavy bodies, so they literally lived off the fat of the land. Whenever possible, their diet included the meat of mammoths and other large animals with abundant fat reserves; even the bones of these animals were prized for their fat-rich marrow. In leaner times, only deer meat or fish might be available, or small reptiles might have to suffice. When the season allowed, berries, wild peas, or cattails from a nearby stream could be eaten right on the spot or taken back to others waiting at the shelter.

Steaks in the Freezer

Woolly mammoths, with fur and flesh intact, have been found frozen in Siberian ice—and their meat is still edible! Neanderthals may have dug up frozen carcasses of mammoths, cut them into chunks with their tools, and defrosted the meat over a fire before cooking it to make a meal rich in energy-laden fat.

A BIG NOSE FOR A COLD WORLD

One of the unique features of a Neanderthal skull is the unusually large nasal cavity in the center of the "face." Considering the size of this cavity, together with the wide sinus cavities behind, we know that Neanderthal noses were enormous—up to four times bigger than ours! And this evidence has led to the conclusion that Neanderthals used their noses to moisten the dry air they inhaled in frigid climates.

When you take a breath, air enters your nose or mouth, travels down the back of your throat through the windpipe and ends up in your lungs. Most scientists agree that Neanderthals breathed in and out through the nose rather than through the mouth. Inhaling cold, arid air through the mouth would have been both painful and dangerous because it would not only dry out the throat lining but possibly cause damage to the lungs as well. Large, mucus-lined nasal passages, however, would have been an adaptation that gave Neanderthals a chance to warm and humidify the air.

Look inside the nasal cavity of a Neaderthal skull and you'll see two triangular projections jutting toward each other from either side. Scientists believe these bony structures provided more surface area for the lining of mucus that warmed and moistened the cold, dry air, preventing damage to the throat and lungs. No other human skull—past or present—contains these odd anatomical features.

Giant-size nostrils would also enable them to take in a greater volume of air, increasing the oxygen supply to every part of their large bodies. And, no less important, they could function as a "thermostat" by expelling hot air to prevent overheating.

Big Nostrils, Big Trouble?

Once temperatures began to climb, the size of their nostrils and the sinuses behind them might have been a drawback instead of an asset for the Neanderthals. Warm air passing through such large, moist areas could lead to severe sinus and upper respiratory infections. In a time when there were no antibiotics or cold pills, infections of this sort could pose a very serious threat to their lives.

In icy climates, Neanderthals breathed through their nose to warm incoming air and let out built-up heat.

Building a Face

We know what Neanderthals' skulls looked like, but what about their faces? Because they left no pictures behind, we have to rely on modern science to complete their portraits for our family album.

One way to fill in a face is to build up a skull with modeling clays, applying less "flesh" to parts like the forehead and more to areas like the cheeks. Next come facial features—eyes, nose and mouth—and finally the finishing touches of skin and hair. We don't know the color of their eyes or skin or how hairy they were, so Neanderthal portraits involve some guesswork. But we can get a pretty good glimpse of the faces that gazed out at the lonely landscapes of the Ice Age.

1. The replica of a Neanderthal skull serves as the base.

2. Muscles and nose cartilage are grafted onto the skull.

3. Eyes and ears are added, and the skin is layered on.

4. A human face emerges as the final touches are applied.

In a computer comparison, an average modern human profile (far left) stretches to fit the larger Neanderthal skull. The image at the near left shows the typical Neanderthal brow ridge, large nose and receding chin.

Computer experts have devised their own methods of building Neanderthal faces. After carefully calculating the different depths of tissue that cover the skull, they "morph," or structure, the face to fit the dimensions. Computers can also be used to build images of complete Neanderthal skulls from fragments. CT-scan technology and 3-D software can fill in all the gaps—even if as much as a third of the skull is missing!

A Leap Across Time

Given a haircut and dressed neatly in a suit, could a Neanderthal sit unnoticed on a modern city bus? Many paleoanthropologists, who study the lives of prehistoric people based on their fossils, believe he'd look familiar enough not to cause alarm among the other passengers.

STANDING UP

The spine, or backbone, is the main support of the human body. Running down the center of the back and protecting the spinal cord, the spine is composed of 24 bones called vertebrae. These ring-shaped bones are separated by disks of cartilage that give the spine flexibility and allow the body to bend and twist.

As hominids evolved and developed an upright gait, changes in their skeletons took place. By the time of the early Neanderthals, the human spine

Some Neanderthal vertebrae show signs of arthritis, a disease that causes bony growths to form at the joints or other places where bones connect with each other. These bony growths, called spurs, would have produced stiffness and swelling in the joints of Neanderthal arthritis victims.

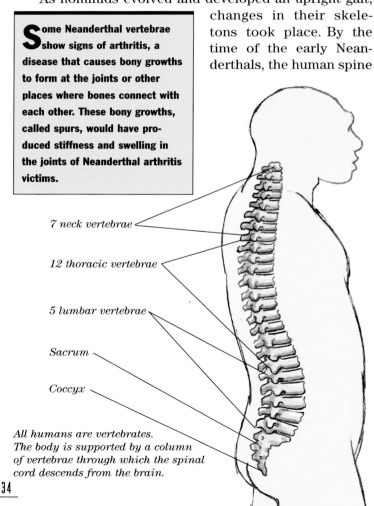

7 neck vertebrae

12 thoracic vertebrae

5 lumbar vertebrae

Sacrum

Coccyx

All humans are vertebrates.
The body is supported by a column
of vertebrae through which the spinal
cord descends from the brain.

had adjusted to the new distribution of weight by assuming the curves of an "S" shape to spread the strain.

Another way we know that Neanderthals walked upright is the placement of the spine on the pelvis. The position of the top of the spine where it meets the skull is also a sign of erect posture. The spine of a four-footed animal, for instance, connects near the back of the skull base, while the human spine joins the skull closer to the center.

The Wrong Picture

In the early 1900s, a French scholar named Marcellin Boule was studying bones from a Neanderthal skeleton called "the Old Man of La Chapelle." From the bones and the way he fit them together, Boule concluded that Neanderthals walked with their knees bent and their big toes splayed out like a chimpanzee's. Their spines, Boule claimed, lacked the curves that allow modern human beings to stand up straight. Based on his description of one skeleton, people back then thought all Neanderthals were shambling, apelike creatures.

What Boule didn't know at the time was that this Neanderthal man was about 30 years old when he died and that he suffered from severe arthritis, which had distorted his bones and fused his spine. In life, "the Old Man" walked with his legs straight and his toes pointed forward, just as we do.

A POWERHOUSE TORSO

The upper body of a Neanderthal was big, strong and well developed. Even the children had wide shoulders, with long collarbones and broad shoulder blades above their barrel-chested torsos. These large bones served as sturdy anchors to which powerful muscles were attached. The shoulder blades supported a greater number of muscles than we have at the same location. In fact, scientists believe Neanderthal shoulder blades were structured different-ly from ours in order to hold special muscles that kept the arms from turning too far during movements that required great surges of strength.

Short, stocky bodies retain heat better than tall, thin physiques. With less skin surface, Neanderthals did not perspire as much as other early humans and therefore retained more heat inside, where it helped to counter the cold temperatures of Ice Age environments.

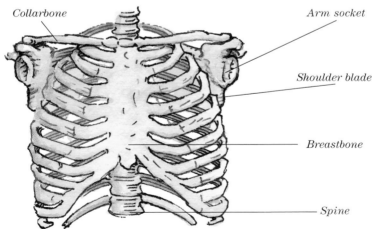

Collarbone

Arm socket

Shoulder blade

Breastbone

Spine

Neanderthals had 12 pairs of ribs, the same number as modern humans, but the rib bones were thicker and heavier. All 12 pairs connected with vertebrae in the spine; only the first 7 pairs were attached to the breastbone in front.

Muscle Men

Ridges and rough patches on fossil bones show where the muscles of the body were once attached. The unusually large size of these attachment points in Neanderthal skeletons indicates the kinds of muscles that we associate with champion weight lifters. One well-known paleontologist speculated that if he had the chest muscles of a Neanderthal man, he would break his ribs if he ever tried to flex them!

Neanderthals used the enormous strength in their upper bodies to defend themselves against dangerous predators and to subdue the large animals they hunted for food.

As in our own bodies, the Neanderthal rib cage not only protected the vital organs in the chest but also worked with the diaphragm to help control the movement of air in and out of the lungs. As the ribs moved up, the chest cavity enlarged and allowed the lungs to fill up with air; when the ribs moved back down, air was forced out of the lungs.

Tough Breaks

Neanderthals lived rugged lives, and injuries to their bones can tell us a lot about the dangers they encountered. One researcher found that Neanderthal men had far more fractures in their skulls and upper bodies than in their lower limbs. Comparing the injury patterns with those of people in active, dangerous jobs today, he found that the Neanderthal injuries were most like those of rodeo riders who frequently get thrown off large animals and are sometimes stomped and gored. Maybe the Neanderthal bone injuries were sustained during the hunt in close combat with the quarry or in life-and-death struggles with fierce predators.

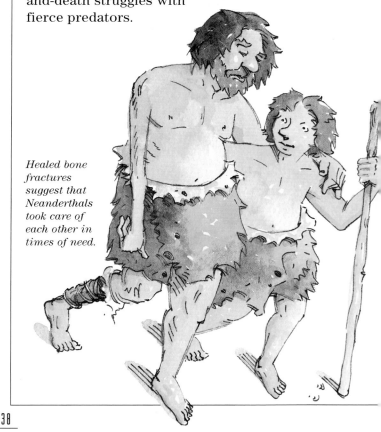

Healed bone fractures suggest that Neanderthals took care of each other in times of need.

Sometimes Neanderthals died of their injuries, but many survived for years afterward. Injured and healed bones of Neanderthal skeletons prove that the sick and injured received at least a minimum of care. The skeleton of a Neanderthal man found at the Iranian site of Shanidar, for example, had a deep groove on his ribs left by a sharp weapon that must have pierced his lung. But he did not die immediately. The wound had begun to heal before he died, indicating that he received help from his extended family while he recuperated.

We know that many fractures in Neanderthal skeletons occurred in life because the bones show signs of healing. Here, a fractured bone has "knit" itself back together again after being broken almost in half.

Another Neanderthal man's skeleton showed many severe injuries before his death. His right arm and shoulder were deformed, and a severe blow to his head had shattered his eye socket. Despite these disabilities, this man lived to be 40—an old age for Neanderthals. Others in the group must have shared food with him and looked after him; otherwise, he would never have survived.

Although most Neanderthals died before the age of 30, a few older-age skeletons have been excavated from caves. Some scientists believe these "elderly" Neanderthals may have been nursed and tended out of respect for their wisdom and experience.

MIGHTY ARMS

Neanderthal arms were short but much more powerful than the arms of modern humans. The extra strength came partly from massive chest and back muscles that moved the arms, but also from the heavy-duty biceps muscles in the upper arms. Working in pairs with the triceps muscle, the biceps bends the arm by pulling upward on the bones of the forearm; the triceps muscle then unbends the elbow and straightens the arm.

Both the arm and the leg have one large bone at the top and two separate, smaller bones below—an inheritance from our ancestors who walked on all fours.

Which Came First?

Did Neanderthals become strong because they used their muscles so vigorously? Or did they lead such active lives because they were born with strong bodies?

Scientists have settled on a combination of the two. In other words, Neanderthals were strong to begin with, and constant exercise developed their bodies even more. One of the best clues comes from the skeleton of a Neanderthal infant whose arm bones were thicker than

The Neanderthal humerus, or upper arm bone, was somewhat bowed and thicker than the humerus in the modern human arm. The slight bow in the bone may have eased the strain of raising the lower arm to lift heavy objects.

Modern human humerus

Neanderthal humerus

those of a modern skeleton at the same age. The points where muscles attached to the bones were also large. So even without having lived long enough to do any lifting, pushing or pulling, this very young Neanderthal was already very strong.

Three Kinds of Joints

Joints are the places where two bones meet in the skeleton. Cushioned by fluid and sometimes soft cartilage, the joints are supported by tough ligaments that fasten to the bones above or below.

Of all the joints in the body, ball-and-socket joints like those at the shoulders allow the greatest range of movement. In the Neanderthal skeleton, these joints were larger than ours to permit the thick, heavy bones to work smoothly.

The strong biceps muscle of the upper arm was capable of bending the arm at the elbow to lift and carry objects that would be too heavy for us without tools to supply the necessary leverage. The biceps muscle also controlled the motion of turning the palm of the hand upward as the wide sliding joint at the wrist allowed the lower arm bones to change position. This powerful structure enabled Neanderthals to pick up rocks, for example, and then turn their hands over to transport them to another location.

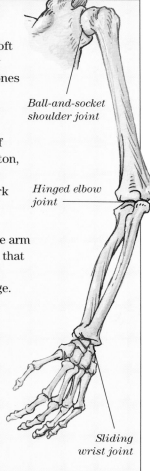

Ball-and-socket shoulder joint

Hinged elbow joint

Sliding wrist joint

SKILLFUL HANDS

With hand bones very similar to ours, Neanderthals could hold objects of many different shapes—from a fistful of pebbles to a tiny plant stem pinched between the thumb and forefinger.

The Neanderthal hand contained the same number of bones as the modern human hand. Below the 8 small bones of the wrist were the 19 hand and finger bones, which were broad and stubby but capable of more dexterity than their appearance suggests. The wide ends of the finger bones met at hinge joints that allowed the fingers to be waggled, cupped and clenched.

The thumb also had a hinge joint, but at its base was a saddle joint that permitted fluid movement—backward and forward, side to side, and even around in a full circle.

Neanderthal finger bones looked a little like the spools used for thread, wider at the ends than through the middle.

It takes 35 strong muscles to move the human hand and fingers—15 muscles in the forearm and 20 in the hand itself. But the size and strength of the bones alone,

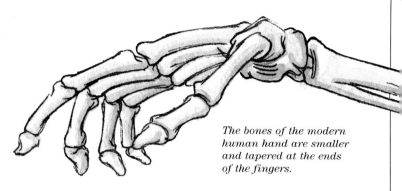

The bones of the modern human hand are smaller and tapered at the ends of the fingers.

coupled with the wide ends of the fingers, gave the Neanderthals a mighty grip that modern humans could never hope to achieve.

In a Pinch

Contrary to early scientific opinion, Neanderthals could perform delicate movements with their hands. Like modern humans, apes and other primates, they had "opposable" thumbs that could touch the tips of all four fingers on the same hand.

This kind of dexterity allowed Neanderthals to use a power grip when force was needed; in other words, they could squeeze an object between the side of the thumb and the palm of the hand. It was also used in picking up small items and manipulating them (the same way we use a pen or pencil today) to fashion the tools they needed in their everyday lives.

The Art of Toolmaking

Archaeological discoveries have shown that early humans made and used a variety of tools for hunting, working animal hides, and preparing and eating food. *Homo habilis*, for example, made simple chopping tools from split pebbles. The Neanderthals, more skilled at toolmaking, devised ways to make flatter, sharper stone chips and to fashion spears and knives by fitting these shaped chips to handles.

Animal bones were plentiful, and they were probably used for tools, but they have not preserved over time. However, the Neanderthals made many of their tools from flint, a fine-grained

Working with Flint

Making tools out of stone wasn't as easy as you might think. Since the use of metals was still a long way off, Neanderthals had to make do with stone, wood, bones or antlers as their toolmaking implements. A stone hammer was the basic tool used for working with flint.

After a promising piece of flint was found, the toolmaker would use a "hammer" to strike a sharp blow and chip away large, thick flakes. For a chopping tool, one edge would have to be smooth and fit comfortably in the user's hand. The working edge would have to be sharp.

Once the basic form of a tool was defined, a light bone or antler hammer was used for chipping off smaller, thinner pieces of flint until the desired shape was achieved. Here, a hand ax is trimmed with the knobby end of an animal bone.

A spear would have been fashioned from stone for the tip, wood for the shaft and animal sinew to attach the tip to the shaft. Possibly a plant gum was also used to "glue" the tip to the shaft.

rock that produces sharp edges when flakes are chipped away by a technique known as "knapping." Since the toolmaker would have to plan just how to strike a rock to achieve a particular shape, scientists believe that the Neanderthals had reached a more advanced level in the art of crafting tools.

Neanderthals also made wooden tools, but very few of these have survived since wood is a material that tends to rot. In 1993, paleoanthropologists in Spain found some shallow wooden dishes that were probably made by Neanderthals. These "bowls" may have been used to carry food or to scoop embers from a fire.

> **F**lint is one of the best stones for making chipped tools. Though very hard, flint flakes easily when struck with another stone or with bone or hard wood. By controlling the angle and size of the flakes, early toolmakers could achieve a wide variety of sizes and shapes.

The Neanderthal Tool Kit

Archaeology is really the study of ancient garbage. While old gnawed bones tell us about a people's diet, tools are evidence of their technology and lifestyle. Excavated sites have yielded a variety of tools that Neanderthals used in their daily lives. Triangular flint knives and spearheads were made specifically for hunting, while flat scrapers served to remove flesh from skins or to cut meat from bones. Tools with thin-bladed points were probably used for piercing holes in hides. And tools with serrated (saw-toothed) edges were most likely fashioned for cutting and planing wood.

> **The techniques used in toolmaking can help scientists understand who made a certain artifact. The period when tools were made solely by flaking is called the Paleolithic period or the Stone Age, which lasted from about 2.5 million years ago to 10,000 years ago—and included the Neanderthal culture.**

Some Neanderthal tools are tricky to identify because they were continually resharpened as they wore down. A large scraper that originally filled the hand, for example, might end up as a small pointed tool to hold in the fingers.

One possible method of attaching a triangular point to a wooden shaft

Chopping tool

Top of the Line

For some of their tools and weapons, Neanderthals used the Levallois technique of striking flakes from modules of flint. In this advanced technique, named for the Paris suburb where it was first pinpointed by archaeologists, the shape of the flake is decided *before* knapping begins and a domed surface is prepared on the module. Within the outline of the striking platform, the flake is then struck off to leave a "tortoise" core.

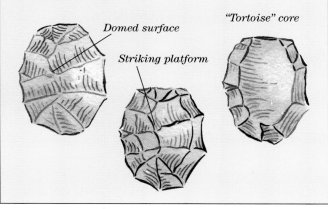

Domed surface

Striking platform

"Tortoise" core

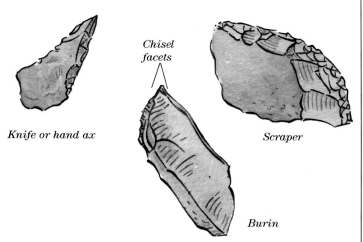

Knife or hand ax

Chisel facets

Scraper

Burin

LEGS FOR HARD LIVING

Looking at the signs of use and wear on Neanderthal leg bones is the next best thing to watching a Neanderthal in motion. Bones become stronger with exercise—and the extra strength of Neanderthal thighbones is clearly seen in their size and shape.

The thighbone, or femur, is the longest, strongest bone in the human body. The upper end fits into the hip socket.

The kneecap bone, or patella, covers the hardworking joint that connects the thighbone to the shinbone (tibia) and calfbone (fibula) below.

All human beings are born with nearly round thighbones, which thicken as time goes by and increasing demands are placed on the bones. People who walk long distances in their daily lives develop a supportive ridge called a pilaster at the back of the bone, where the stress is greatest. A similar ridge is evident in the Neanderthal thighbone, but it's accompanied by thickening along the part of the bone that faces the outside of the leg. Such added support indicates that Neanderthals lived action-packed lives, climbing up and down, lunging from side to side, and stretching their bodies to the limit.

The bones of the lower leg have something to tell us about Neanderthals, too. Neanderthal shinbones often have grooves in their surfaces called "squatting facets." These marks result from the strain placed on the bones by squatting in the same place for long periods of time. Neanderthals probably hunkered down to make tools, prepare food—or just take a well-deserved rest!

The thighbones of Neanderthal children tell us that the whole family followed an energetic way of life. When children are very active, the knobby ends of these bones tend to bend at the point where they meet the hip bones. The ends of juvenile Neanderthal thighbones are more sharply bent than any modern child's, showing that youngsters learned to scramble early on to keep up with the adults.

It's not just muscle that becomes stronger with exercise—bone becomes thicker and stronger, too.

STEPPING OUT

Neanderthal feet looked and functioned very much like modern human feet. The bones in the feet help keep the rest of the body balanced and push off from the ground to move it from one place to another. The arch near the center of the foot acts like a shock absorber to cushion the jolt that each step produces.

Neanderthal feet consisted of the same number and configuration of bones, but the bones were thicker and the joints larger than ours. The thick toes with their extra gripping power were helpful in climbing up and down the rocky sides of cliffs.

The human big toe is the "motor" that moves the body forward. Tree-dwelling primates, which do not walk upright, use their big toes like thumbs to take hold of branches and other objects that humans would need their hands to grasp.

The remarkable discovery of a single preserved footprint gives us a picture of the way Neanderthals walked—and it wasn't that different from our own way of walking. In the footprint, the heel, the ball of the foot and the sturdy toes all sank deeply into the ground, while the arch of the foot pressed more lightly. The deepest imprint of all was left by the big toe, the last part of the foot to leave the ground.

The human foot contains 26 bones: 14 in the toes, 5 in the instep and 7 in the ankle. Although the feet have as many muscles and joints as the hands, they have less freedom of movement but far more strength.

Strong Ties

Neanderthal skeletons required a system of super-strength cords not only to move the bones but also to fasten them to each other.

Ligaments as heavy as rope tied one bone to another where they met at the joint, providing a secure connection even when the two bones were in motion. Five of these ligaments were needed to hold the ankle joint together.

Tough *tendons* woven into the bone tissue were attached at one end to muscles; sliding up and down inside a sheath of fiber like an arm inside a coat sleeve, they allowed the muscles to move the bones by pulling on them. The large Achilles tendon, for example, connected three of the calf muscles to the heel bone at the back of the foot.

Calf

Achilles tendon

Ankle ligaments

Heel bone

Foot bones

The next time you walk barefoot on soft ground or along a sandy beach, take a look at your own footprints. You'll find that just for an instant, with every step you take, your big toe supports the whole weight of your body.

The Hunt Goes On

Broken, cut and smashed bones of animals found at the sites tell us that Neanderthals ate meat. But how did they get it? Did they know about the seasonal migrations of herds, or was hunting simply a hit-or-miss event that took place whenever they needed food? And what about the evidence suggesting that a lot of their food came from scavenging the kills of animal predators?

Many cave sites have yielded proof that Neanderthal hunters brought down big game—the animals' bones bear the cut marks made by stone weapons. Hunting large animals called for group planning, especially if spears were the only weapons. Neanderthals had to know which animals to hunt, where the animals were, where to stand and how to kill them. Fossil evidence indicates that some hunters stampeded herds over cliffs and sometimes forced animals into bogs or shallow ponds.

The meaty ribs and thighbones of animals are often missing from Neanderthal caves, indicating that the found bones may have been retrieved from other animals' prey. Chances are, Neanderthals

Piles of bones discovered at the bottom of steep cliffs suggest that hunters deliberately stampeded big animals to their death below.

The larger animals were probably butchered on the spot and chunks of meat wrapped in the skin for transporting. Smaller carcasses were likely carried over the shoulders back to the shelter.

took advantage of food resources whenever and wherever they could. If they happened upon a cave lion enjoying a kill, perhaps they did what they could to take advantage of the find, such as chasing the lion away.

A Bone to Pick

Bones of small mammals are rarely found at Neanderthal sites, but most scientists agree that small animals could have been a main part of their diet. Why aren't the cave sites peppered with tiny bones? Possibly these animals, because they were small, were eaten on the spot and not brought home to the cave. On the other hand, these bones were so small and fragile they may have been trampled or crushed into the ground and not preserved for future finds.

A TELLTALE PELVIS

The bony bowl called the pelvis protects the lower organs of the torso and supports the spine. In modern humans, the two pubic bones that meet in front of the bowl are short and stubby, but in Neanderthals these bones were surprisingly long and slender. In addition, the opening within the pelvis was positioned farther forward than ours, placing the center of gravity directly over the hip joints on either side. This slightly different structure may support the view that Neanderthals did less

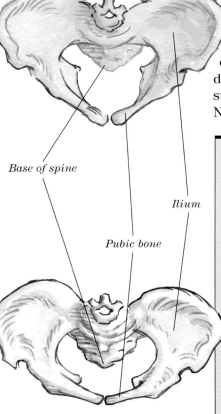

Neanderthal pelvis

Base of spine

Ilium

Pubic bone

Modern human pelvis

The shape of the pelvis is important because the walking muscles are attached to it. The human pelvis is short and wide, while the pelvis of an ape is tall and narrow. Apes can take a few steps on two legs, but they bend at the hips and rock from side to side on wide-apart feet. Human feet fall closer together, under the center of the body, so walking is a more natural endeavor.

straightforward distance walking than the early *Homo sapiens* and moved in a more roundabout manner as they performed their daily activities.

The Littlest Neanderthals

Before a complete pelvis was discovered, scientists thought the Neanderthals' long, thin pubic bones were designed to make a larger birth canal. Neanderthal babies would then have been able to grow larger than modern human babies before they were born and would be better equipped to survive in the tough Ice Age environment. But the complete Neanderthal pelvis had a "normal"-size opening, so it's safe to assume that babies developed inside their mothers for only nine months—the same as modern babies.

Neanderthal babies were stronger than modern human babies of the same age, but most never lived to become adults. Bones of Neanderthal babies, children and teenagers found in caves and rock shelters outnumber those of adults. Life during the Ice Age was tough.

THE NEANDERTHAL WAY OF LIFE

We know that Ice Age environments could be harsh, and that many groups of Neanderthals kept warm in caves and other places of refuge that nature provided. But did they stick close to the same cave or travel from one shelter to another in their constant search for food, flint and firewood?

More than likely, climate and geography encouraged both life-styles. There are even hints that some Neanderthals made crude, tent-like shelters from slender tree trunks and animal skins. Mammoth tusks and leg bones have also been discovered at a site where they might have served as supports for the roof of a primitive hut.

Ancient holes found at Neanderthal sites indicate that poles were set into the ground to support primitive tents. Saplings would be leaned against a horizontal ridge pole at the top.

Animal skins would be hooked onto branch stubs or lashed with thongs. The bottom layer of skins would then be weighted down with stones.

The Neanderthal Way of Life

Bundling Up

Not one scrap of their clothing has survived, but the Neanderthals must have used something to cover themselves in cold weather. Tools as well as worn-down teeth recovered from Neanderthal sites provide a few important clues. The stone scrapers would be ideal for removing traces of flesh and fat from an animal skin, while rounded teeth show signs that they might have been used for chewing on hides to soften them.

Adding up the evidence, it seems highly probable that Neanderthals wrapped themselves in bearskin or other animal hides. But it's unlikely that they sewed the hides into shirts or leggings since the oldest bone needles date from about 26,000 years ago—too late for the Neanderthals. Maybe they slit the hides and wore them like ponchos. Perhaps they pierced holes in the hides and laced them together with rawhide thongs.

On the other hand, Neanderthal needles might still be out there, waiting to be discovered!

Day by Day

It's hard to know how Ice Age people spent their days and nights. But from bits of animal bones, ashes, flint and pollen, scientists can reconstruct a scene of Neanderthal community life. Members of the extended family must have spent their days hunting and gathering food, preparing meals over a fire, eating and cleaning up, and making tools and weapons. Early Neanderthals scooped out the cave floor to make a simple fireplace; later on, more formal hearths were built with circles of stones.

Life in a cave community revolved around the necessities for survival—food, water, warmth, and a collection of basic tools and weapons.

Gnawed and charred bones, along with vestiges of seeds and pollen, have been discovered piled up against the back walls of cave dwellings. These "garbage heaps" indicate that Neanderthals kept separate living spaces where they performed their daily routines.

Flakes of flint arranged in patterns around areas of ash found at cave sites show where Neanderthals chipped patiently by the fireside. Perhaps, by the warmth and comfort of a fire, men spoke among themselves as they worked with stone, while women kept busy preparing animal skins and keeping an eye on the children.

RITES AND RITUALS

Did Neanderthals have religious beliefs? We may never know, but interesting evidence can be found among their bones.

Flower Power

In 1960, scientists found a Neanderthal male skeleton surrounded by clusters of pollen from spring flowers. There was far too much pollen to have settled by accident or been carried by animals. This was a gravesite, and flowers must have been placed on and near the body after death. The spring-blooming plants of bachelor's buttons, hollyhocks and grape hyacinth suggest the time of year when the man died. And the pollen suggests something even more intriguing. Most of these plants are used today by people of the region to make poultices or herbal remedies. Were the flowers intended to restore him to health in the afterlife?

A number of Neanderthal skeletons have been discovered lying on their side and with the knees bent. Often they are found in scooped-out pits, covered by earth

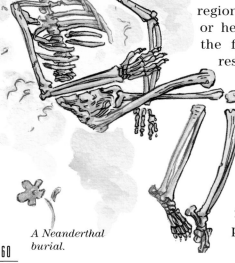

A Neanderthal burial.

of a different color from the surrounding soil. The survivors must have dug shallow graves, arranged the dead bodies and covered them with earth. These burials show that at the very least, Neanderthals valued each other and thought that a dead person deserved respectful treatment.

The grave of a 10-year-old Neanderthal child was found in 1992. On the pelvis of the small skeleton was the jaw of a red deer. Why was the jaw there? Was the red deer a special animal protector of the child? Could its placement have a religious significance?

> Some Neanderthal bones have been found with cut marks on them. The cuts are too straight to have been caused by animal teeth or claws; likely they were made by flint tools. Other bones are broken in a way that suggests the marrow was scooped out of them. These clues may indicate the practice of cannibalism. Maybe the Neanderthals were starving—and they ate only those who had already died of hunger. Or maybe they ate parts of a person who had been revered in life as a way of incorporating some of his or her good qualities.

Curious Ruins

In 1996, a strange structure was discovered deep inside an underground cavern. Built with broken stalactites and stalagmites, it's in a place so far away from sunlight that the builders must have used torches to light their way.

Scientists have traced the structure back to Neanderthals. But they cannot answer the question "Why?" Was it a place of worship? A place for secret rituals? No one knows. What the presence of the structure does tell us is that this is the first evidence that Neanderthals knew how to carry fire from one place to another. But researchers still have no idea what the structure was and why it was built so far from daylight.

ECHOES FROM THE PAST

Did Neanderthal hunters shout to each other above the wind that swept over the tundra? Were soft voices heard around the evening fire inside the caves?

The 1983 discovery of a tiny hyoid bone among Neanderthal remains proved that these early humans were capable of speaking. Only an inch and a half long,

Let's Talk!

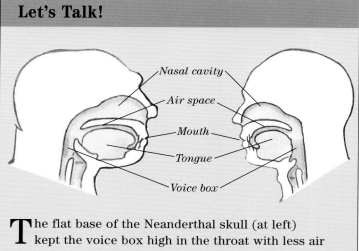

Nasal cavity

Air space

Mouth

Tongue

Voice box

The flat base of the Neanderthal skull (at left) kept the voice box high in the throat with less air space than the modern human skull (right) allows for producing sounds.

the hyoid bone supports the voice box, or larynx, which produces the sounds of speech. The Neanderthals probably didn't make all our vowel sounds (a, e, i, o and u), and they may have used fewer consonants. But most scientists agree that they communicated with each other in a language that helped them work together and live in harmony.

The Sounds of Music

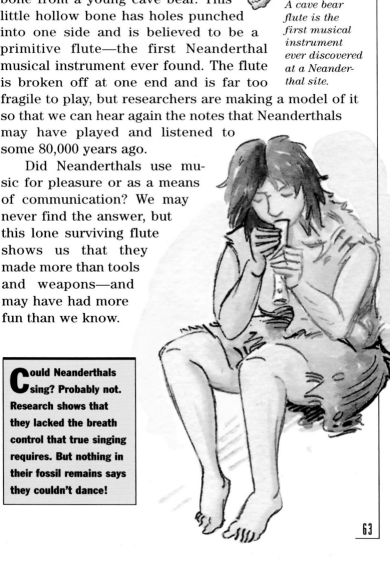

Another piece of the Neanderthal puzzle was discovered in 1996, when paleontologists came across a four-inch-long section of thighbone from a young cave bear. This little hollow bone has holes punched into one side and is believed to be a primitive flute—the first Neanderthal musical instrument ever found. The flute is broken off at one end and is far too fragile to play, but researchers are making a model of it so that we can hear again the notes that Neanderthals may have played and listened to some 80,000 years ago.

A cave bear flute is the first musical instrument ever discovered at a Neanderthal site.

Did Neanderthals use music for pleasure or as a means of communication? We may never find the answer, but this lone surviving flute shows us that they made more than tools and weapons—and may have had more fun than we know.

Could Neanderthals sing? Probably not. Research shows that they lacked the breath control that true singing requires. But nothing in their fossil remains says they couldn't dance!

What Happened?

One thing we know for sure is that the Neanderthals disappeared about 30,000 years ago. Archaeological sites dating to this time period are plentiful, but what archaeologists find is evidence of modern humans—not Neanderthals. What doomed the robust and large-brained Neanderthals to extinction after survivng the worst climates of the Ice Age?

Being strong and robust didn't guarantee success in the changing conditions at the end of the Ice Age. Did the Neanderthals need to eat more than modern humans to survive? Were their big bodies less well adapted? Or were the modern humans who lived at the same time better organized and better able to plan for the future?

Are we the answer? Archaeologists have found no evidence of fighting, although that could have happened. We know Neanderthals and modern humans lived near each other in the same parts of the world for tens of thousands of years. They may have traded hunting or toolmaking techniques and could perhaps have communicated in some fashion. They may have shared animal and plant resources in the same valleys, but never lived together or interbred.

Were we better hunters? Did a greater ability to communicate help us to develop more effective ways of living together in groups? Were the brains of modern humans better organized for planning and adaptive, creative thinking? We simply don't know. Probably the answer to the extinction of the Neanderthals is a combination of things: changing climate and food resources, small population, and being outcompeted by a species better suited to the times.

New discoveries will add to our collection of clues. Keep watching and reading! With each find, we learn more about the life and death of the Neanderthals—and a little bit more about ourselves.